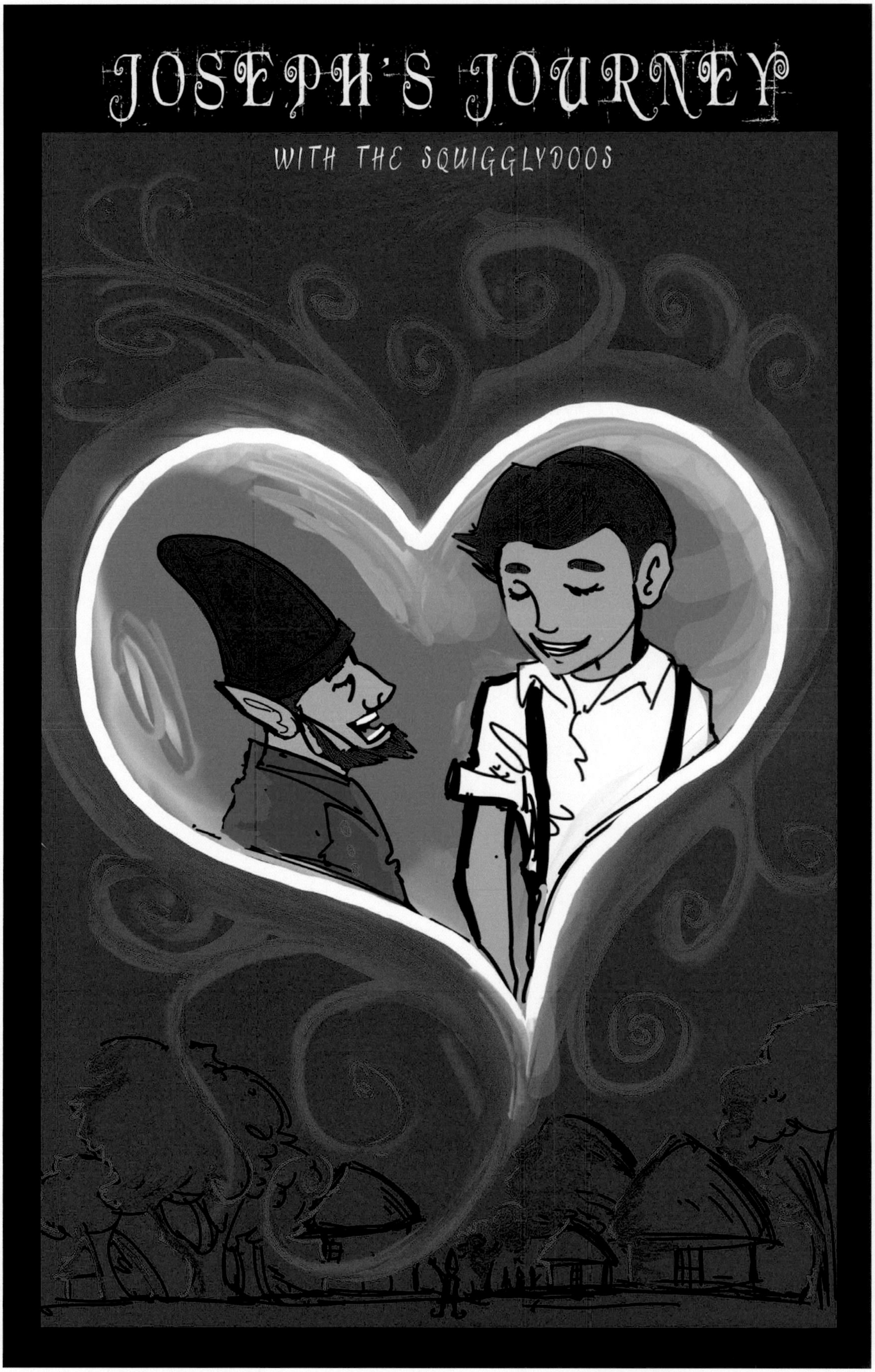
JOSEPH'S JOURNEY
WITH THE SQUIGGLYDOOS

DUNCAN WATSON

AuthorHouse™ UK
1663 Liberty Drive
Bloomington, IN 47403 USA
www.authorhouse.co.uk
UK TFN: 0800 0148641 (Toll Free inside the UK)
UK Local: 02036 956322 (+44 20 3695 6322 from outside the UK)

Because of the dynamic nature of the Internet, any web addresses or links contained in this book may have changed
since publication and may no longer be valid. The views expressed in this work are solely those of the author and do not
necessarily reflect the views of the publisher, and the publisher hereby disclaims any responsibility for them.

Any people depicted in stock imagery provided by Getty Images are models,
and such images are being used for illustrative purposes only.
Certain stock imagery © Getty Images.

This book is printed on acid-free paper.

ISBN: 978-1-6655-8296-4 (sc)
ISBN: 978-1-6655-8295-7 (e)

Print information available on the last page.

Published by AuthorHouse 12/19/2020

authorHOUSE®

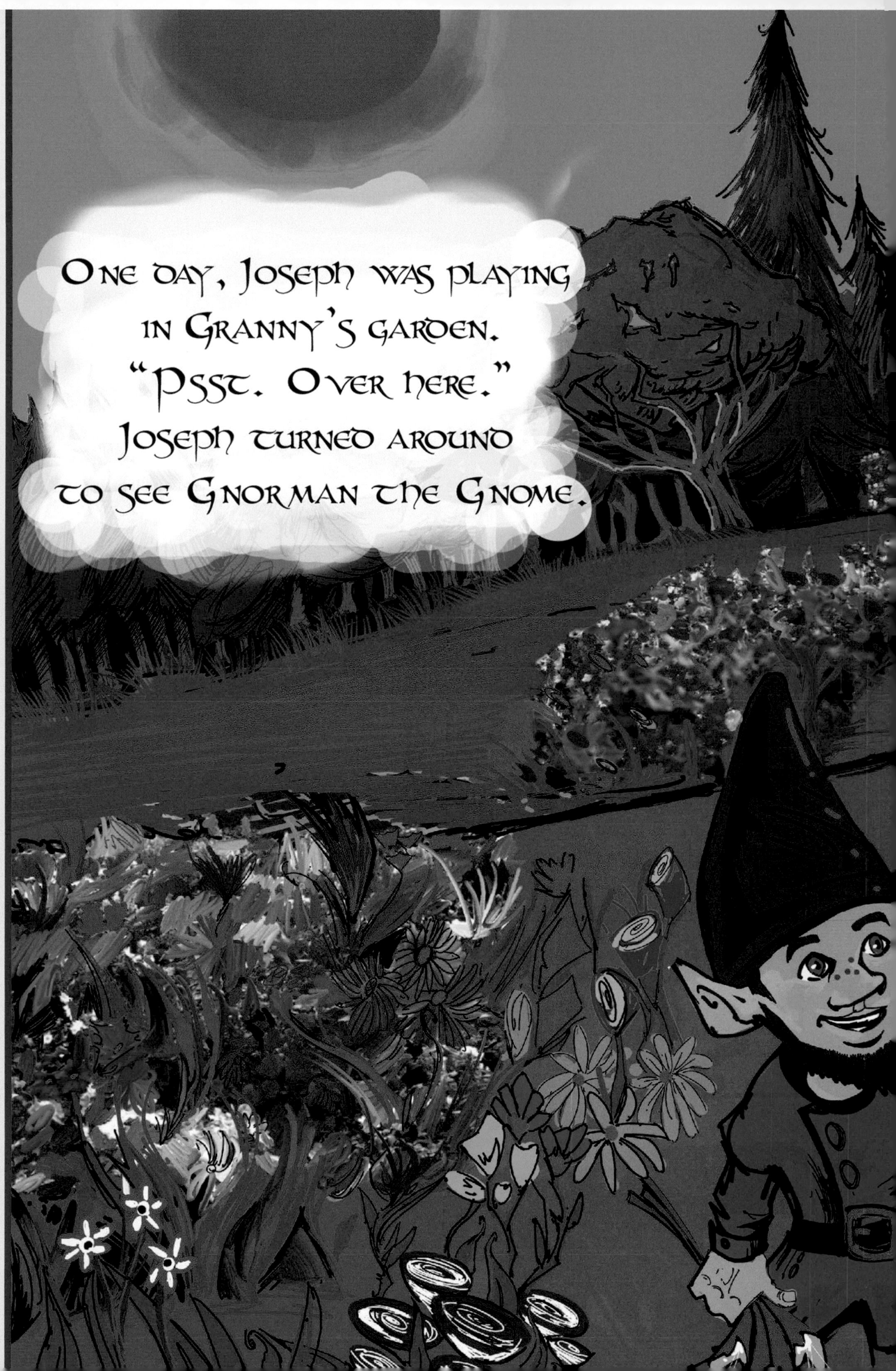
One day, Joseph was playing
in Granny's garden.
"Psst. Over here."
Joseph turned around
to see Gnorman the Gnome.

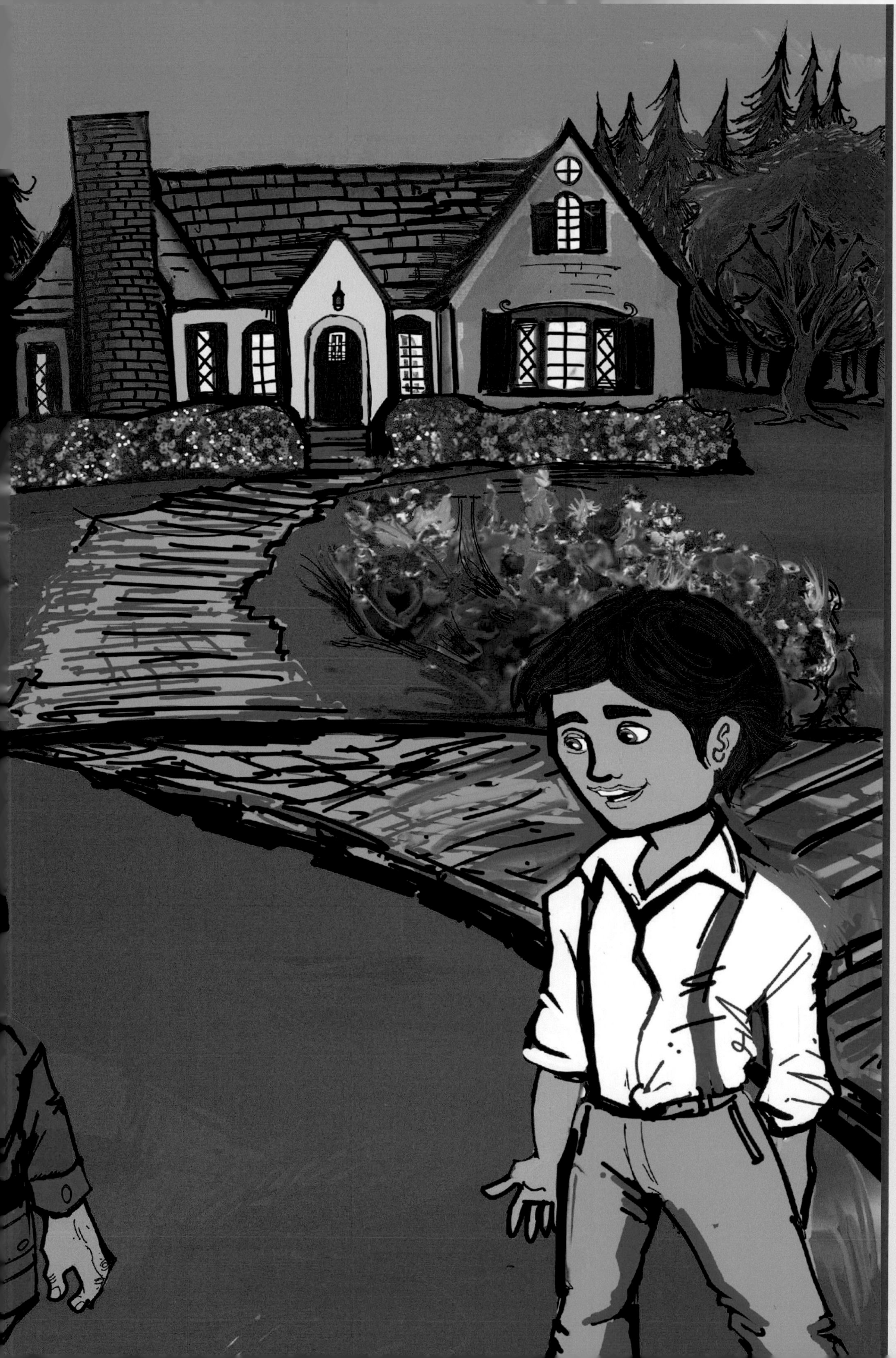

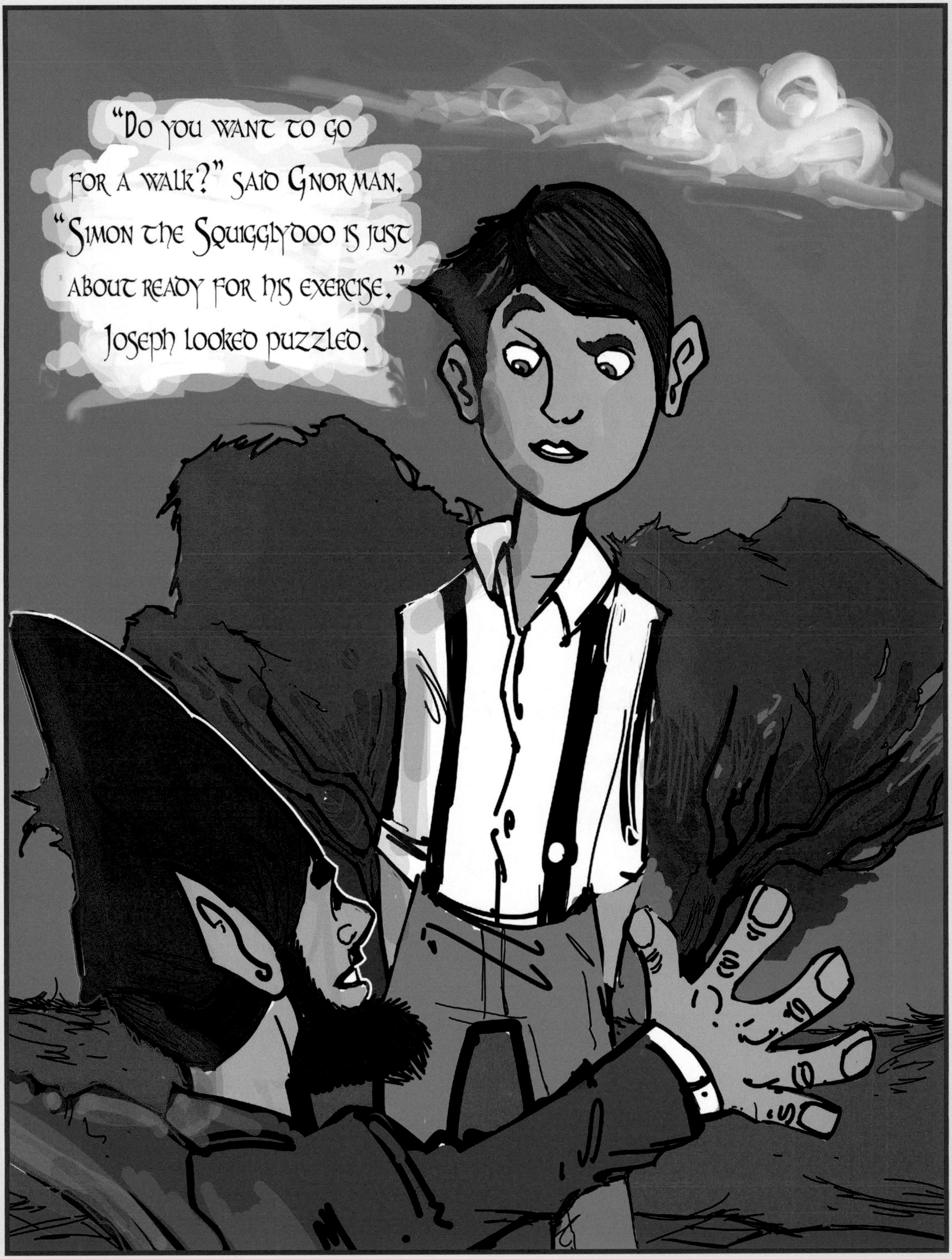
"Do you want to go
for a walk?" said Gnorman.
"Simon the Squigglydoo is just
about ready for his exercise."
Joseph looked puzzled.

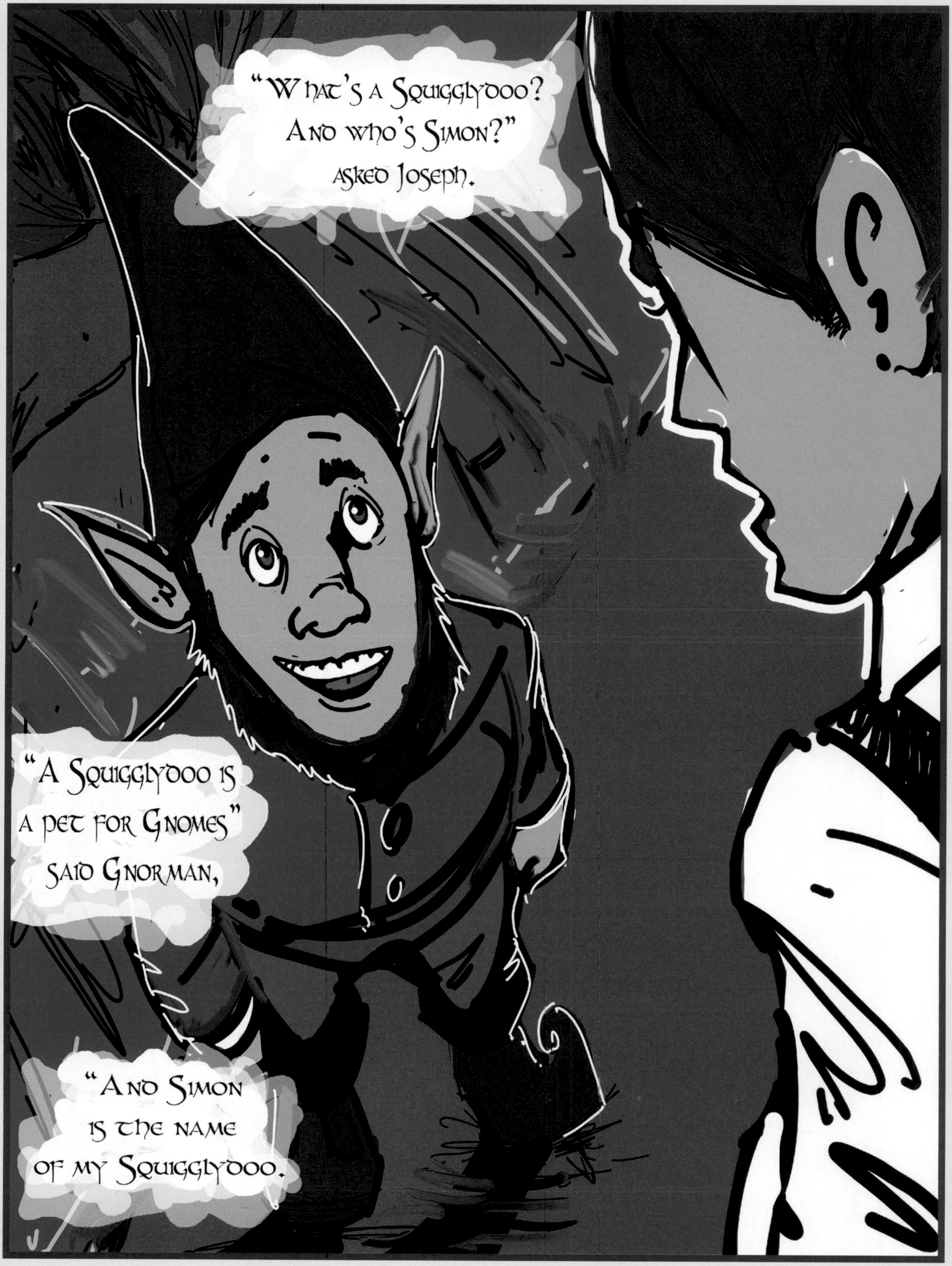
"What's a Squigglydoo? And who's Simon?" asked Joseph.
"A Squigglydoo is a pet for Gnomes" said Gnorman,
"And Simon is the name of my Squigglydoo.

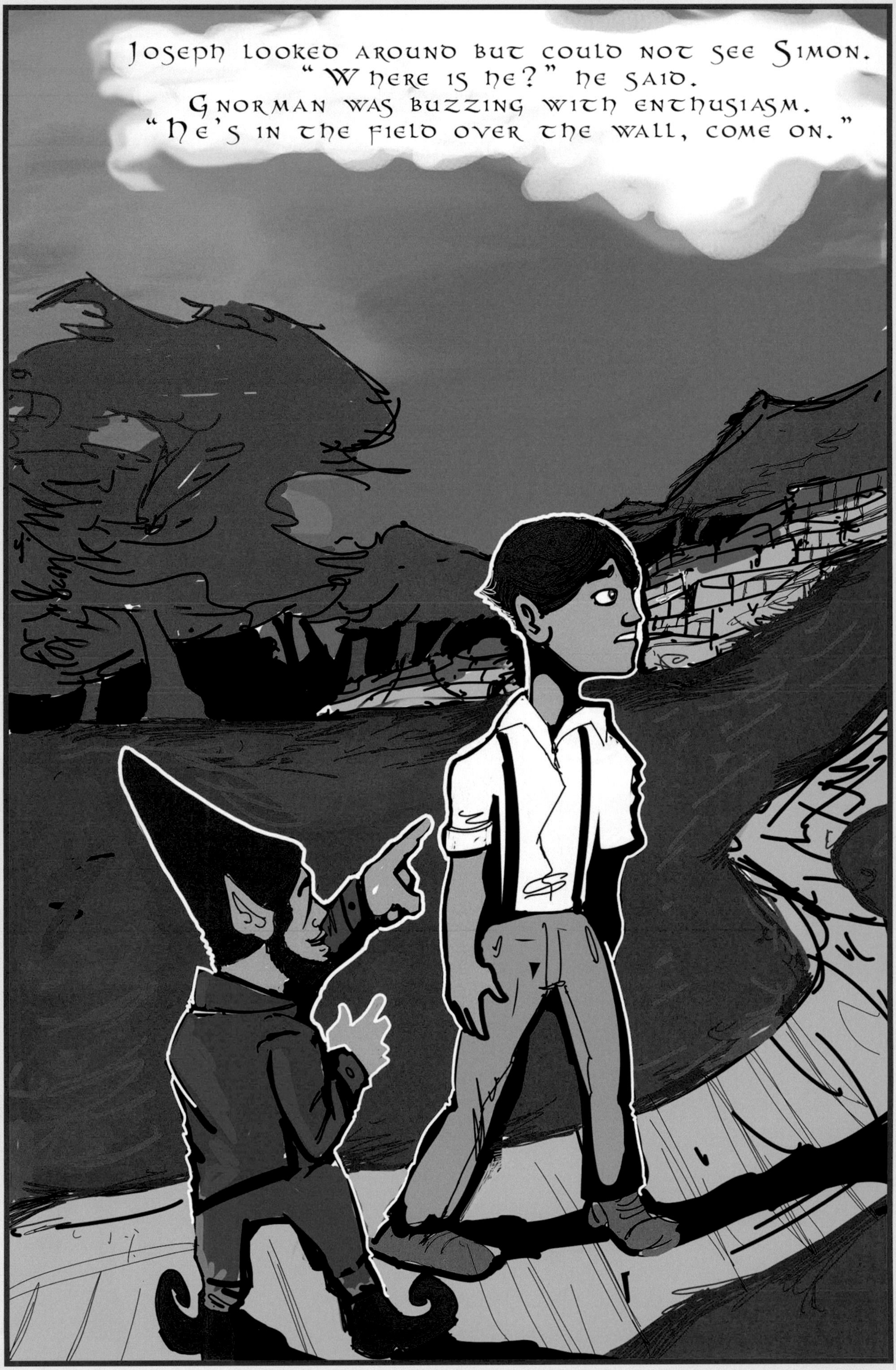
Joseph looked around but could not see Simon.
"Where is he?" he said.
Gnorman was buzzing with enthusiasm.
"He's in the field over the wall, come on."

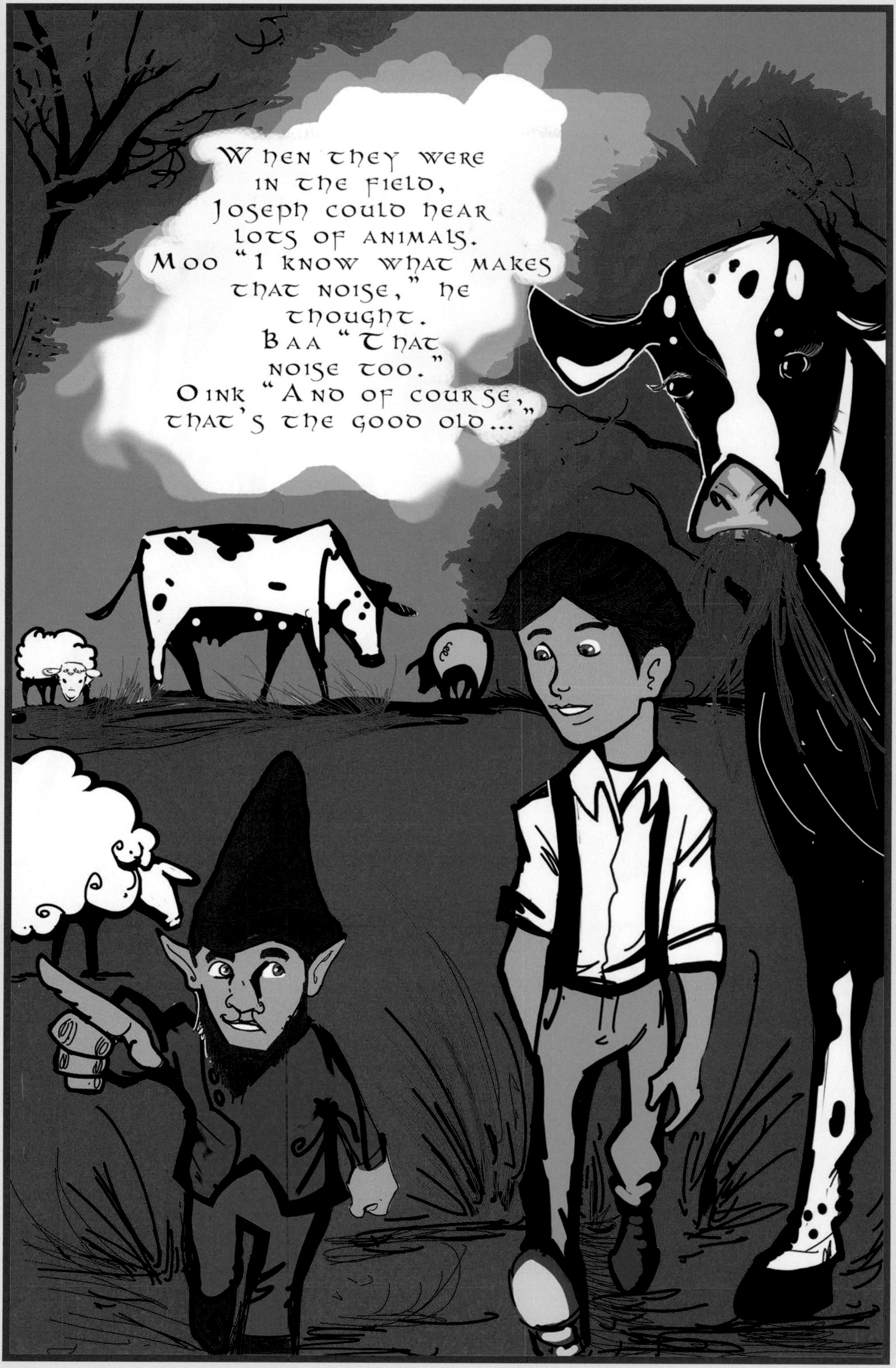
When they were
in the field,
Joseph could hear
lots of animals.
Moo "I know what makes
that noise," he
thought.
Baa "That
noise too."
Oink "And of course,
that's the good old..."

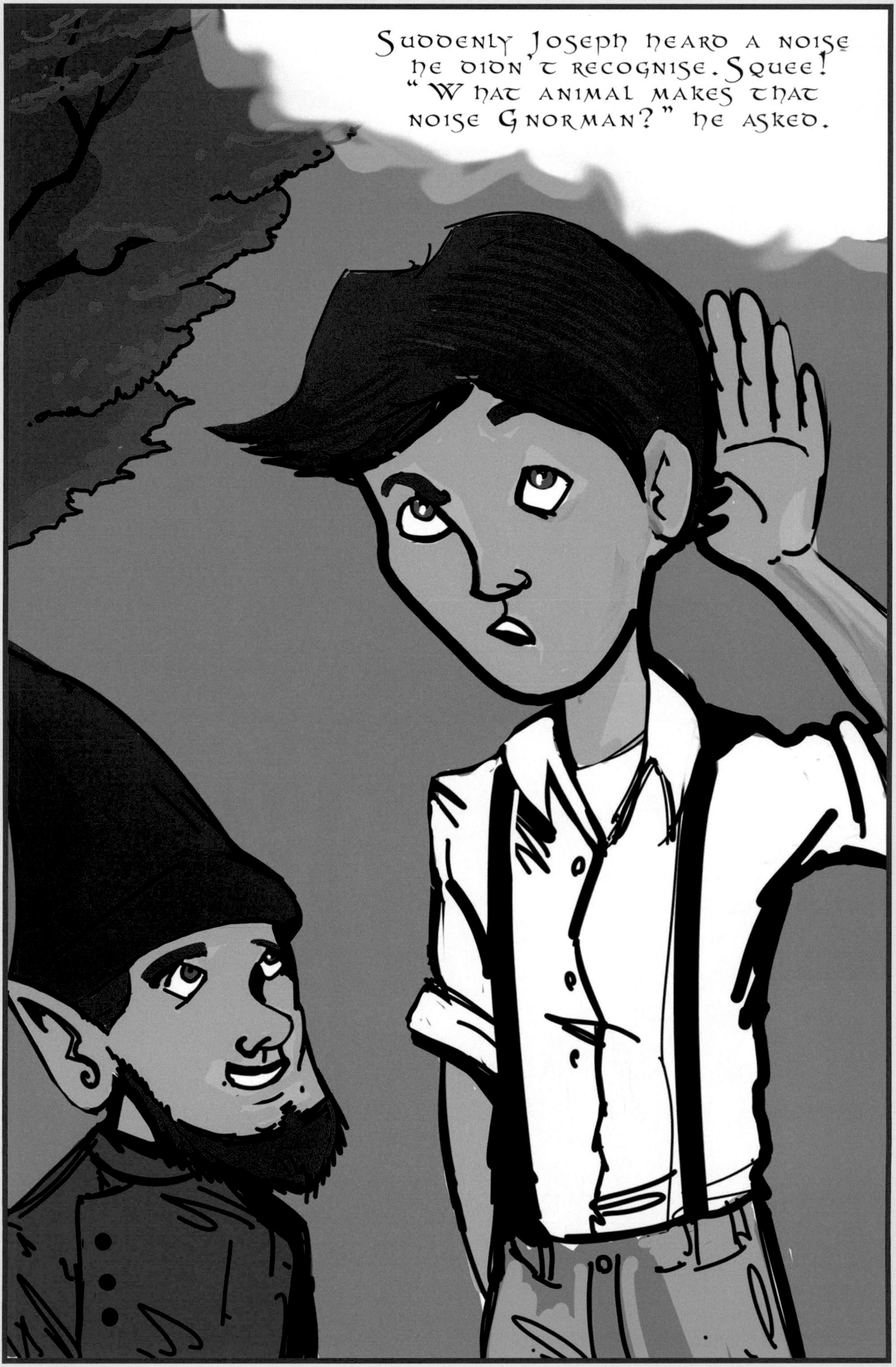
Suddenly Joseph heard a noise he didn't recognise. Squee! "What animal makes that noise Gnorman?" he asked.

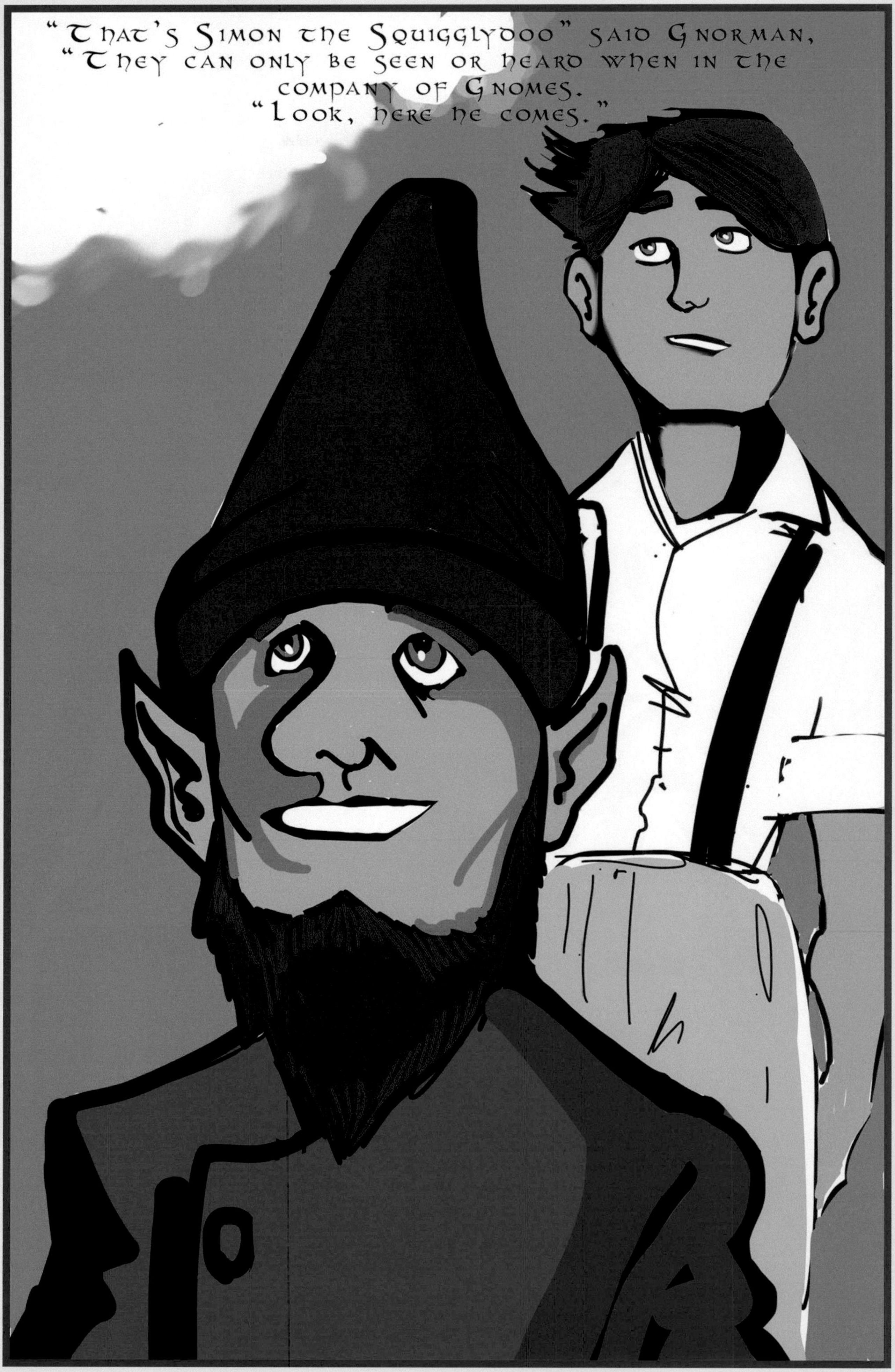
"That's Simon the Squigglydoo" said Gnorman,
"They can only be seen or heard when in the company of Gnomes.
"Look, here he comes."

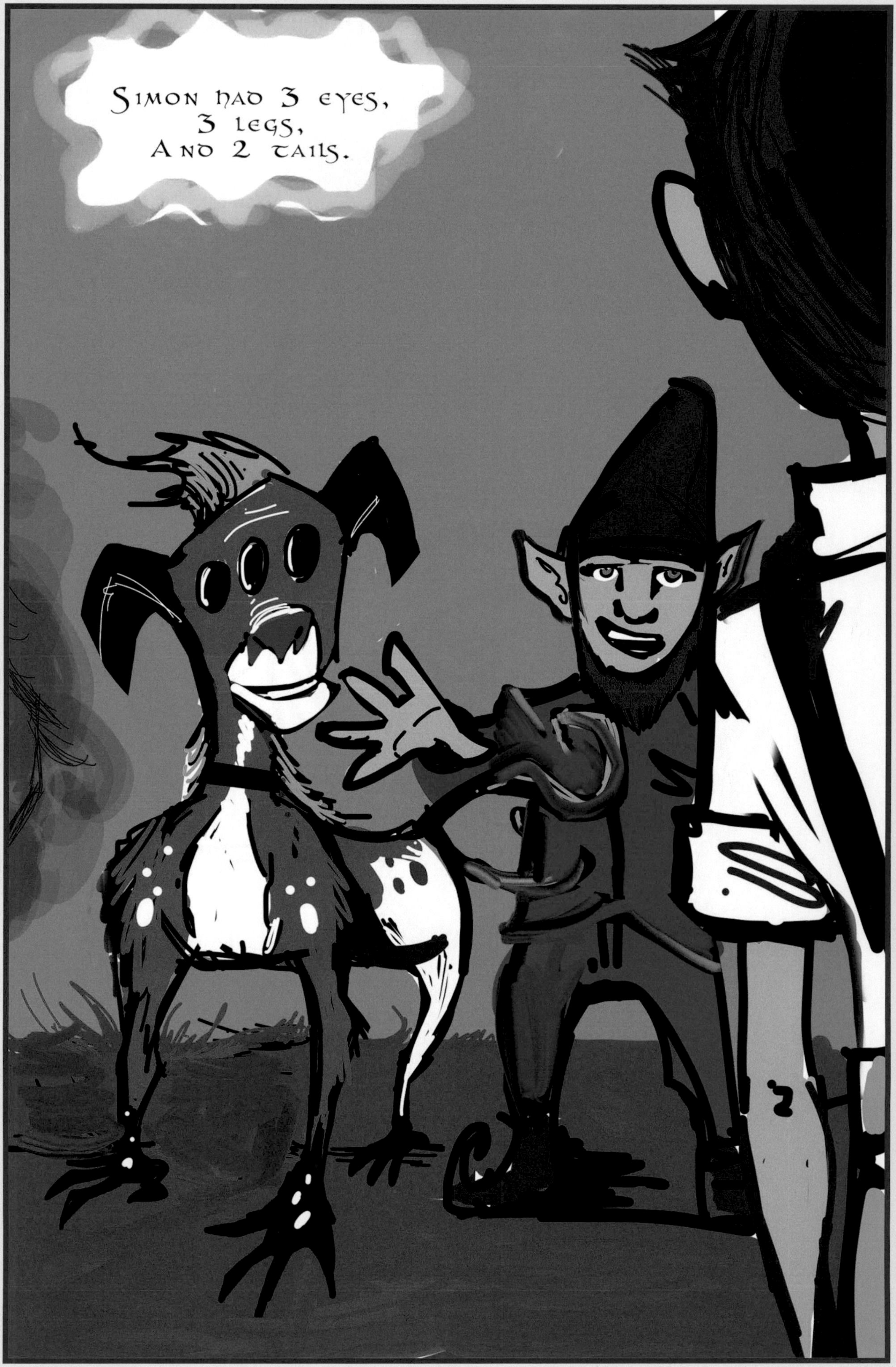
Simon had 3 eyes,
3 legs,
And 2 tails.

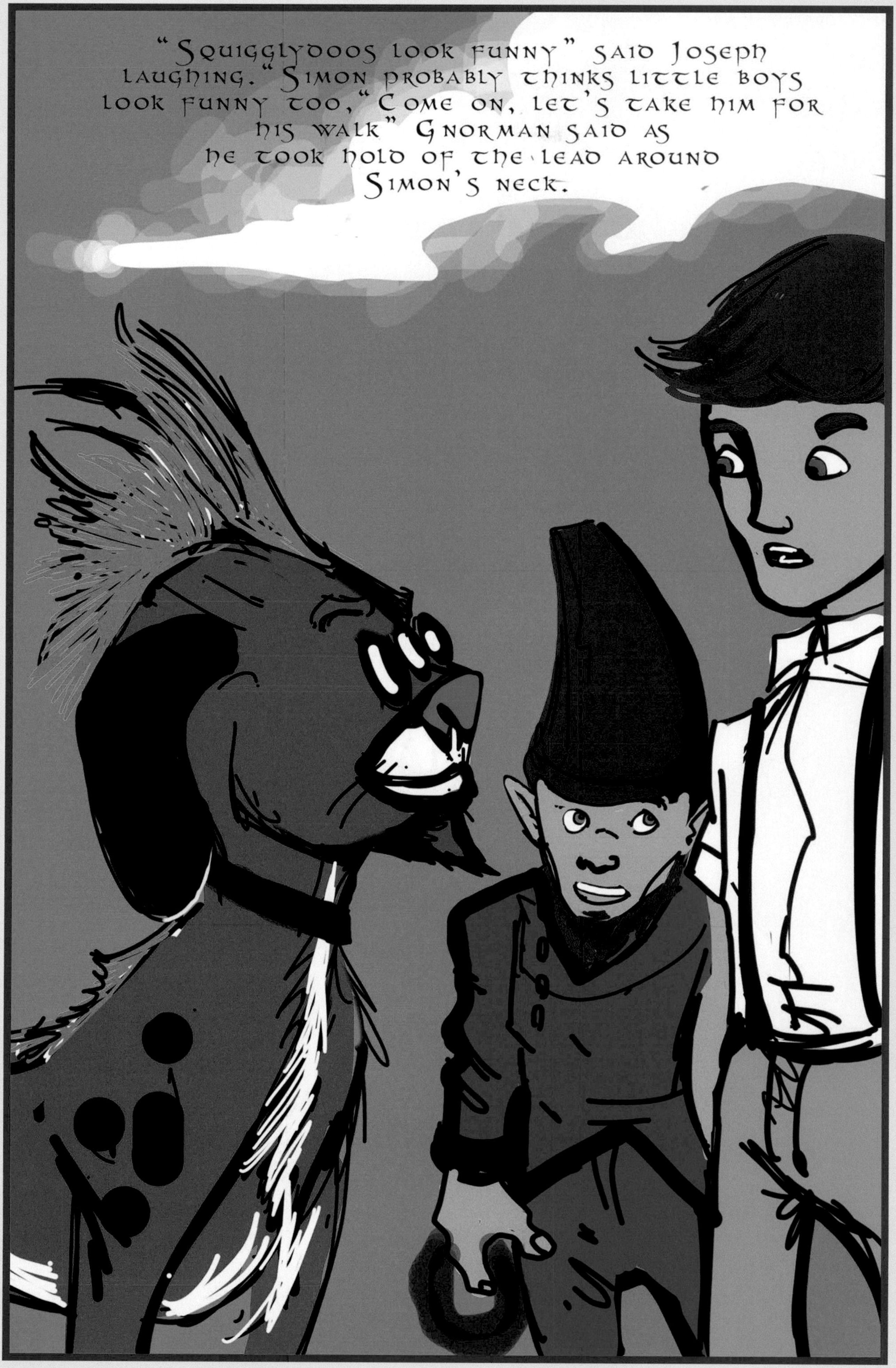
"Squigglydoos look funny" said Joseph
laughing. "Simon probably thinks little boys
look funny too," "Come on, let's take him for
his walk" Gnorman said as
he took hold of the lead around
Simon's neck.

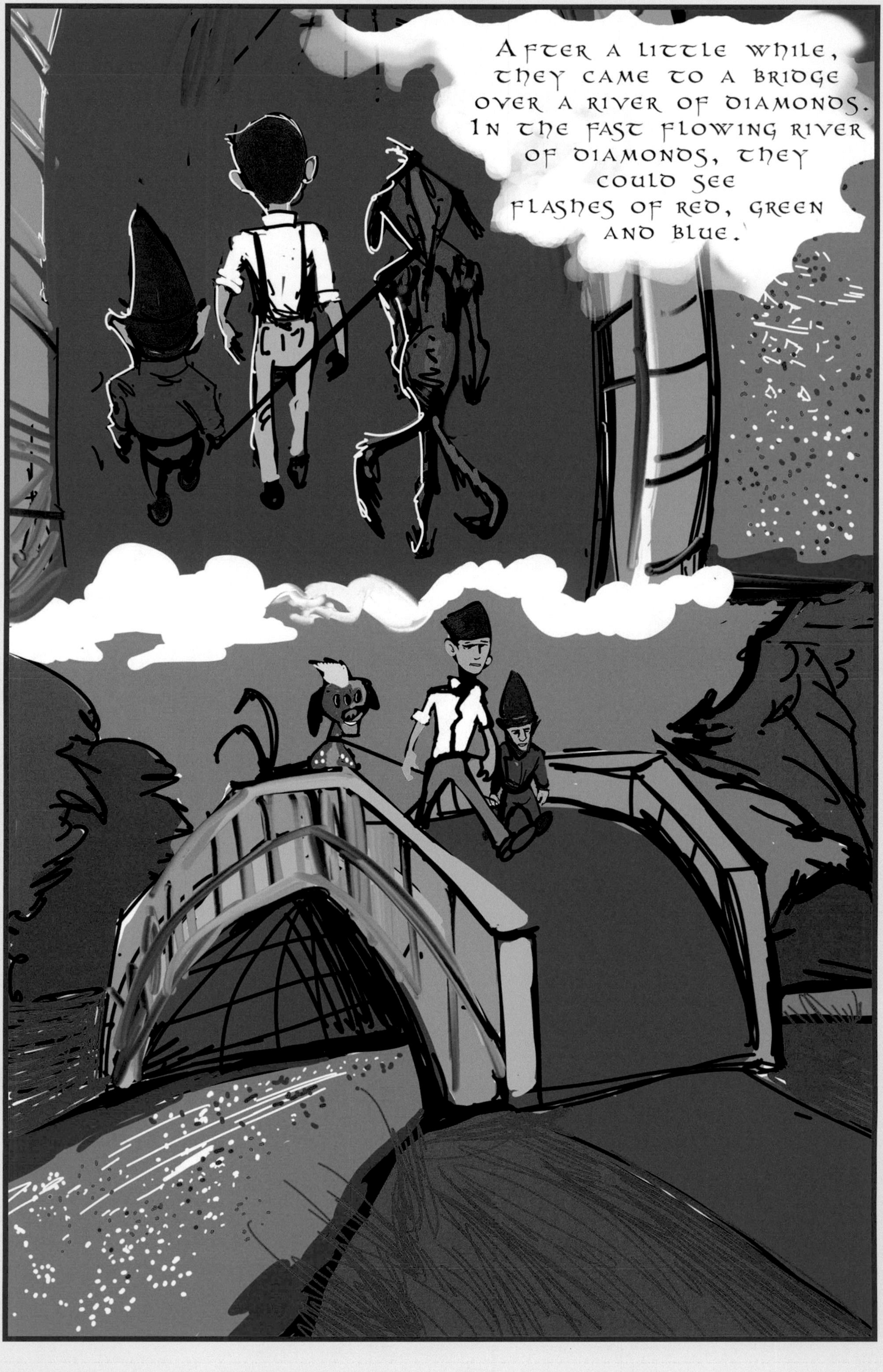
After a little while, they came to a bridge over a river of diamonds. In the fast flowing river of diamonds, they could see flashes of red, green and blue.

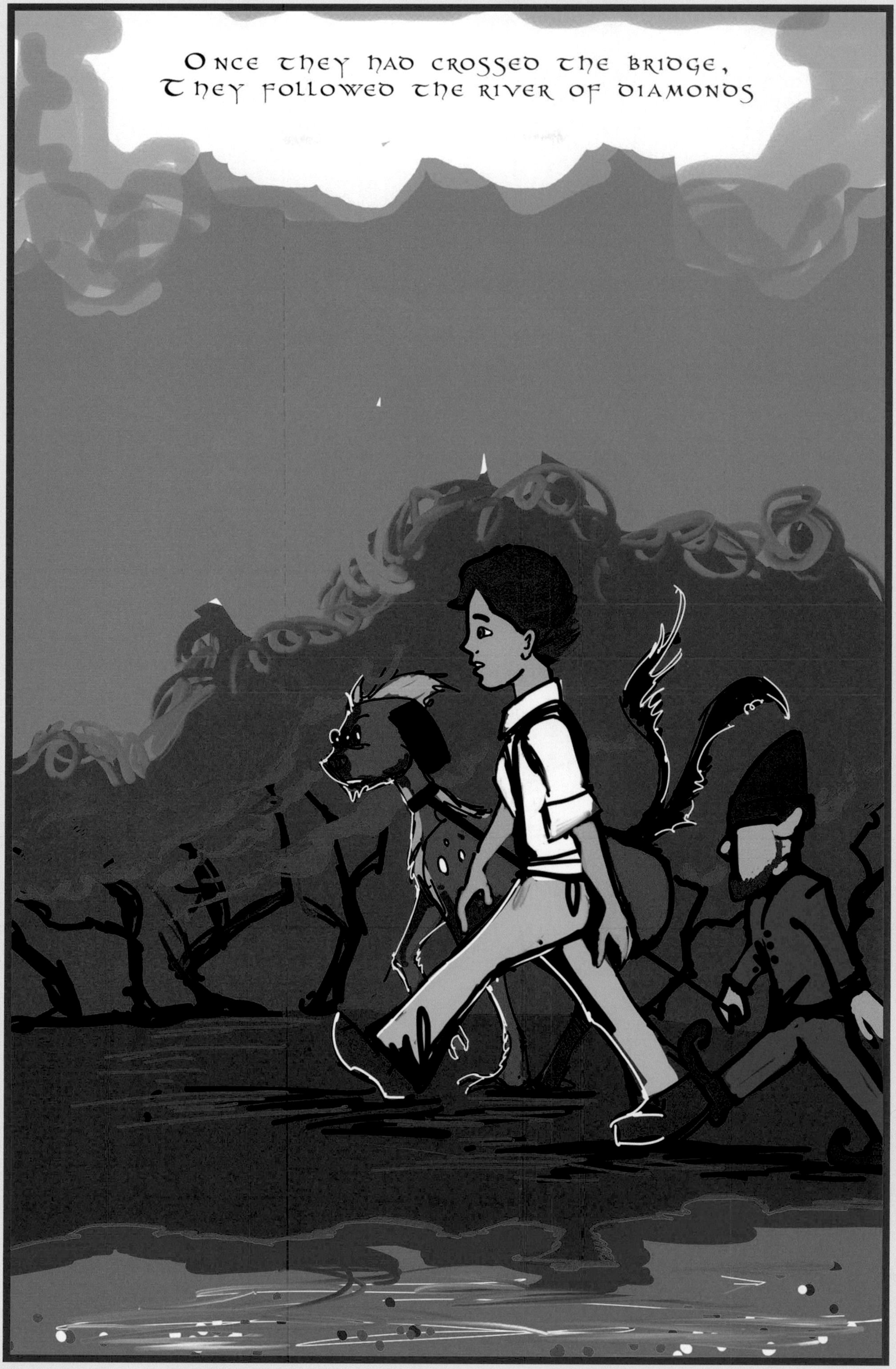
Once they had crossed the bridge,
They followed the river of diamonds

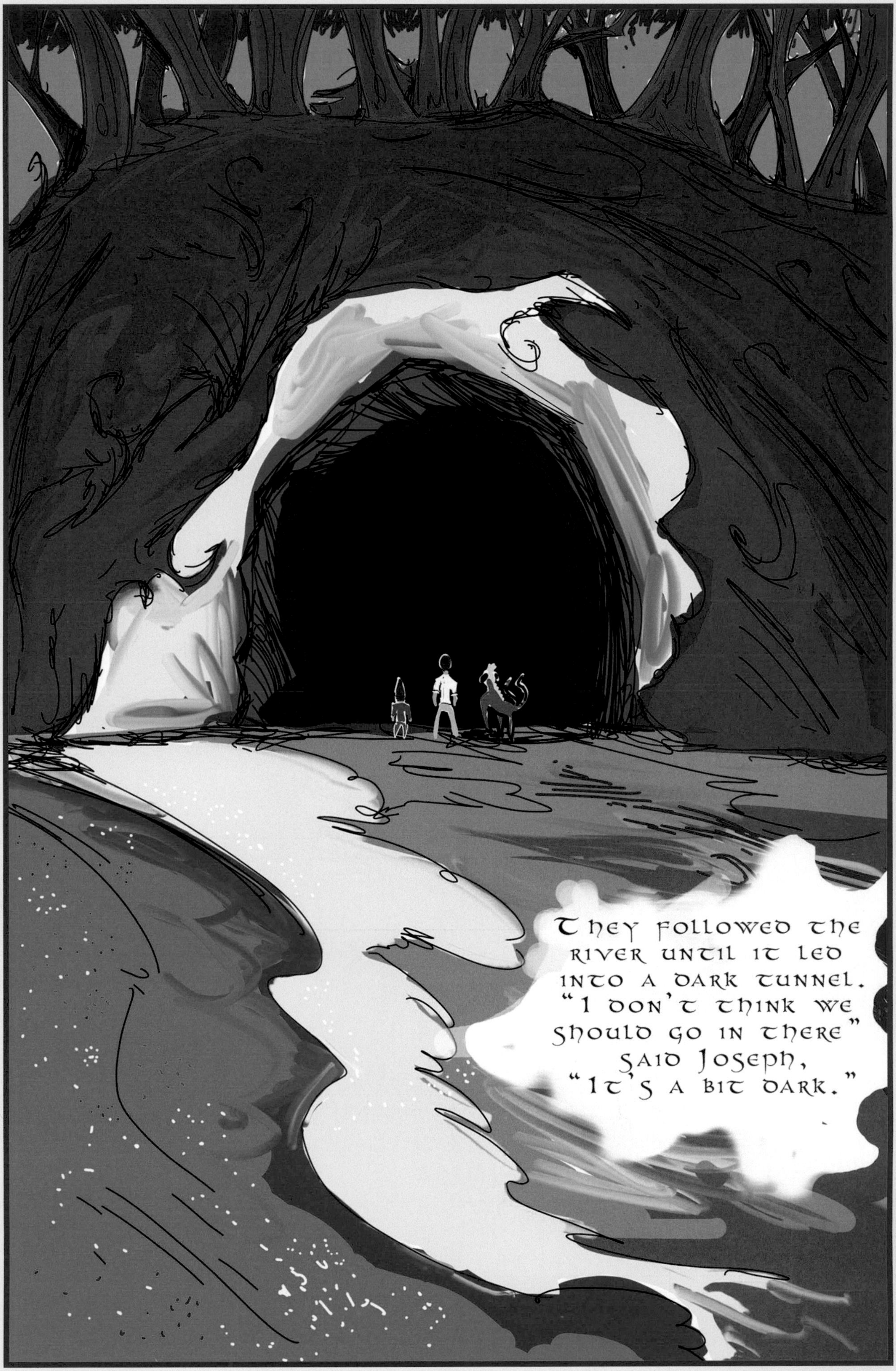
They followed the river until it led into a dark tunnel. "I don't think we should go in there" said Joseph, "It's a bit dark."

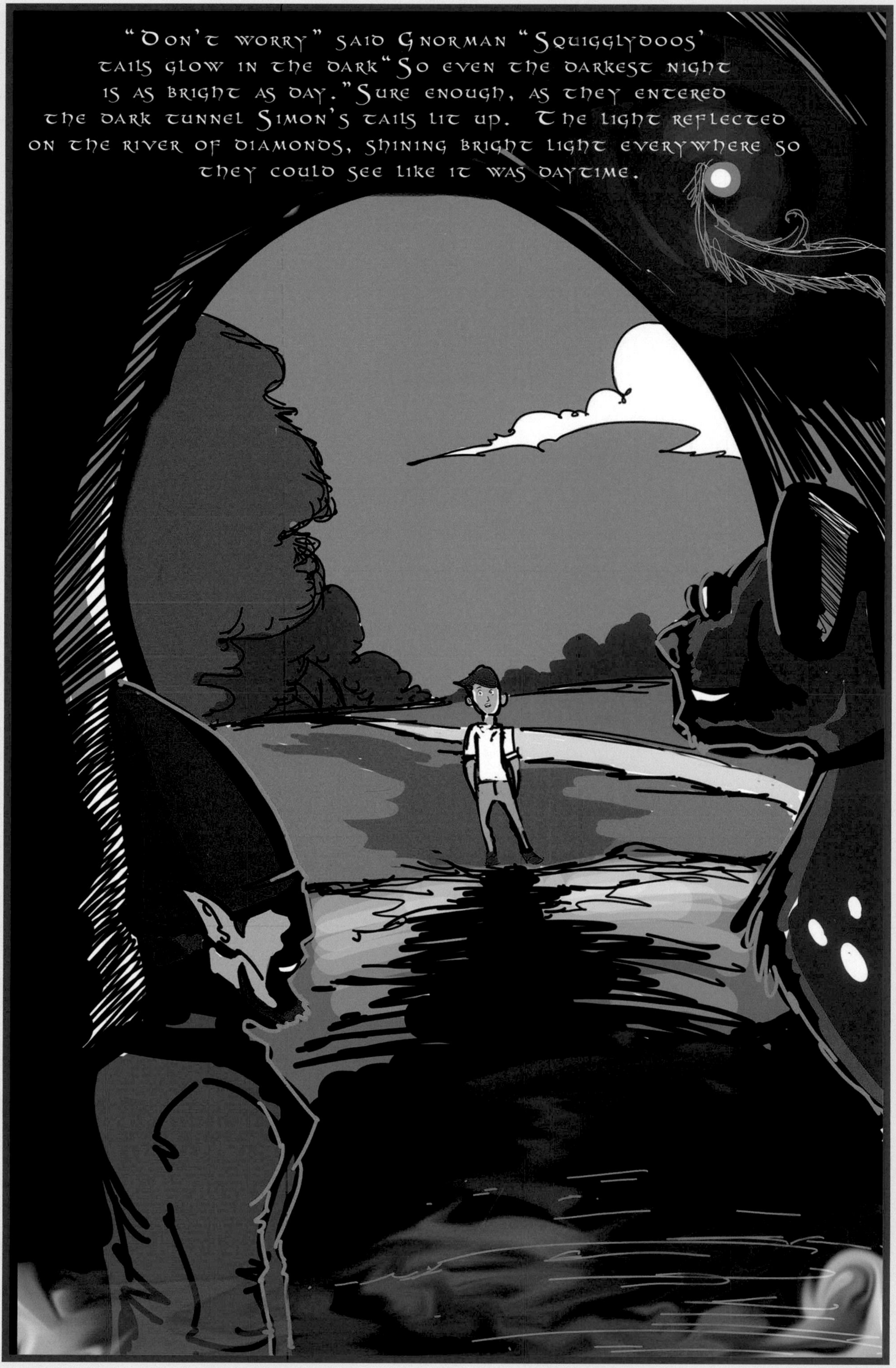
"Don't worry" said Gnorman "Squigglydoos' tails glow in the dark"So even the darkest night is as bright as day."Sure enough, as they entered the dark tunnel Simon's tails lit up. The light reflected on the river of diamonds, shining bright light everywhere so they could see like it was daytime.

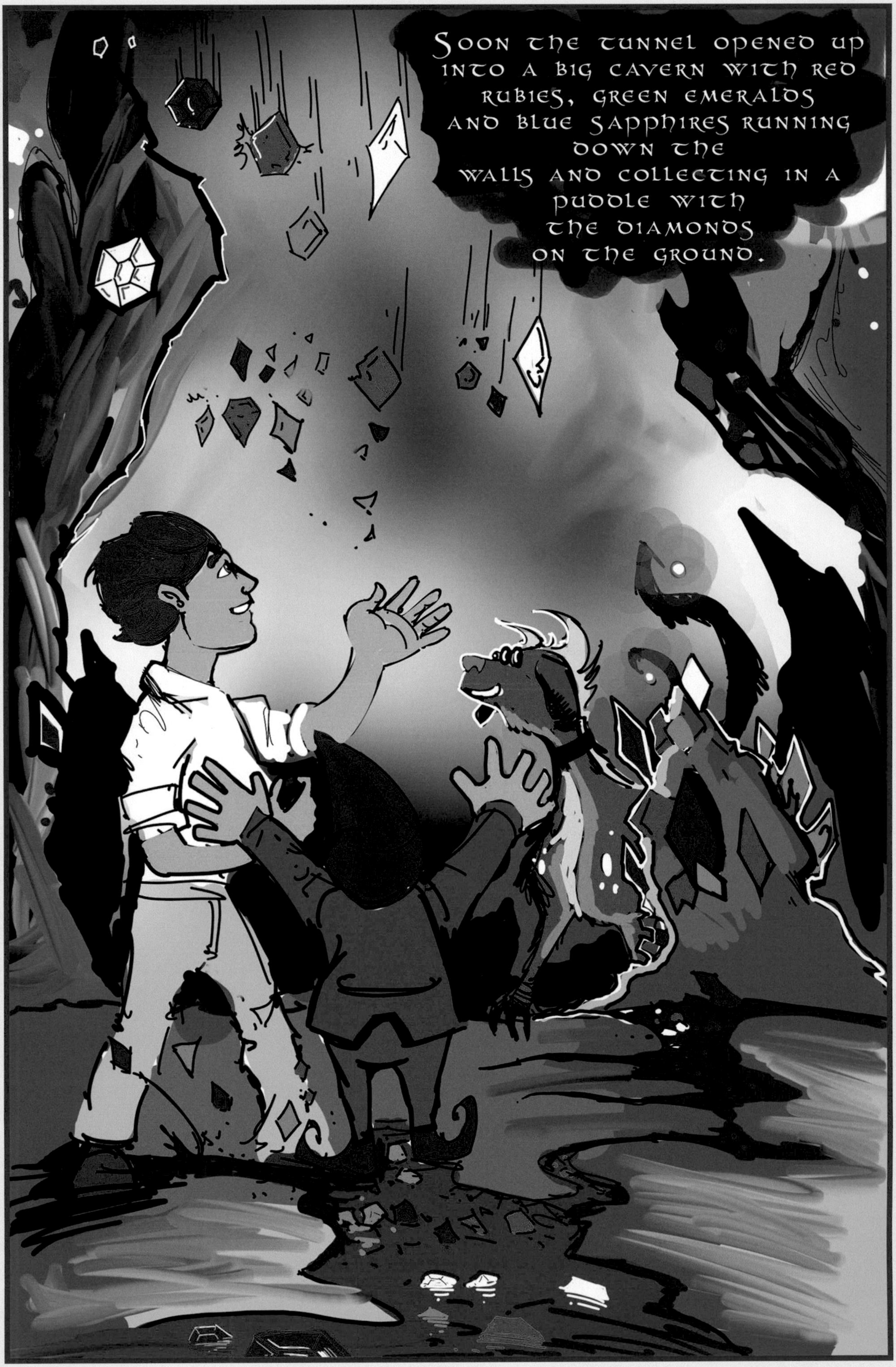
Soon the tunnel opened up into a big cavern with red rubies, green emeralds and blue sapphires running down the walls and collecting in a puddle with the diamonds on the ground.

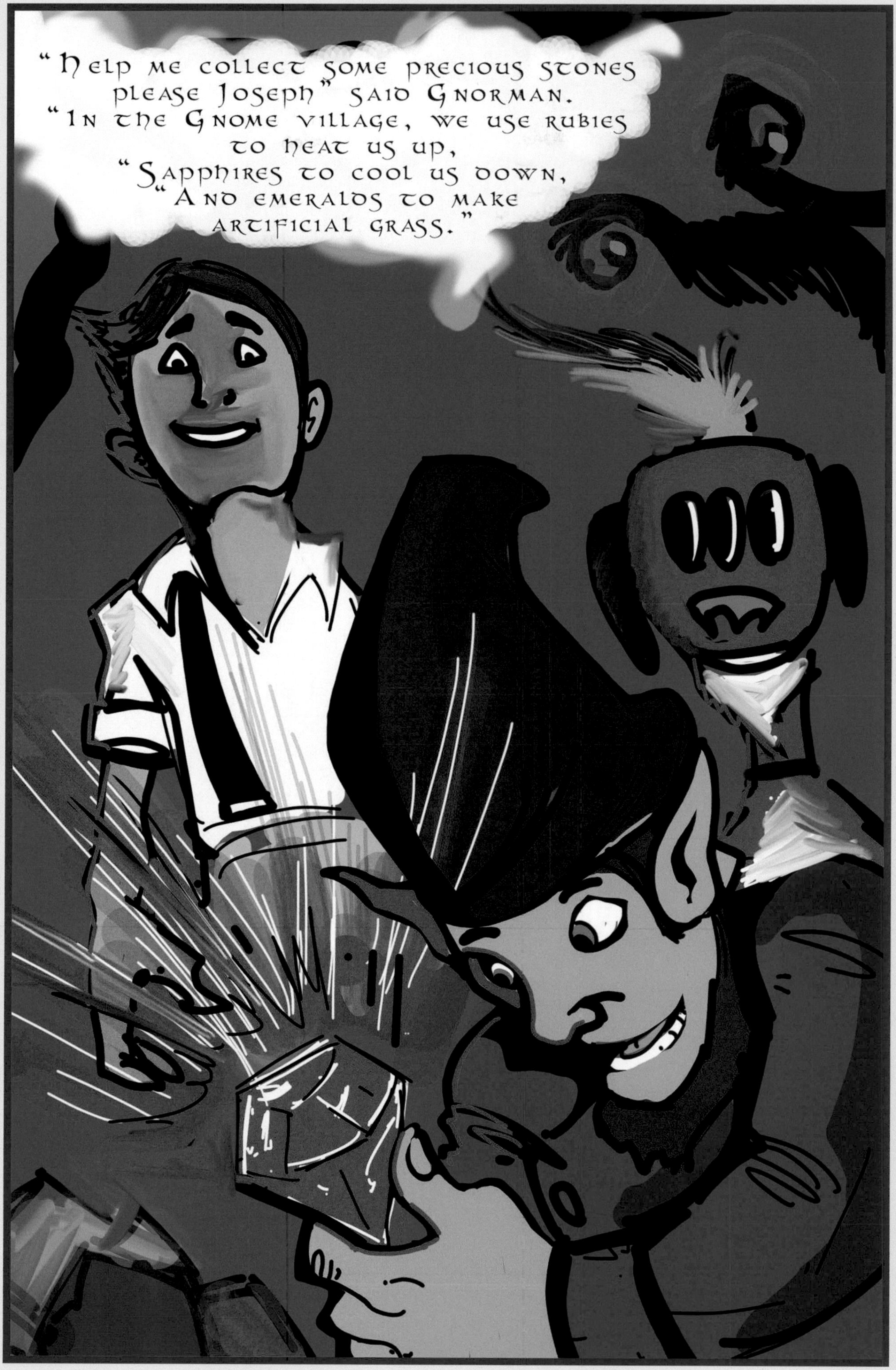
"Help me collect some precious stones please Joseph" said Gnorman.
"In the Gnome village, we use rubies to heat us up,
"Sapphires to cool us down,
"And emeralds to make artificial grass."

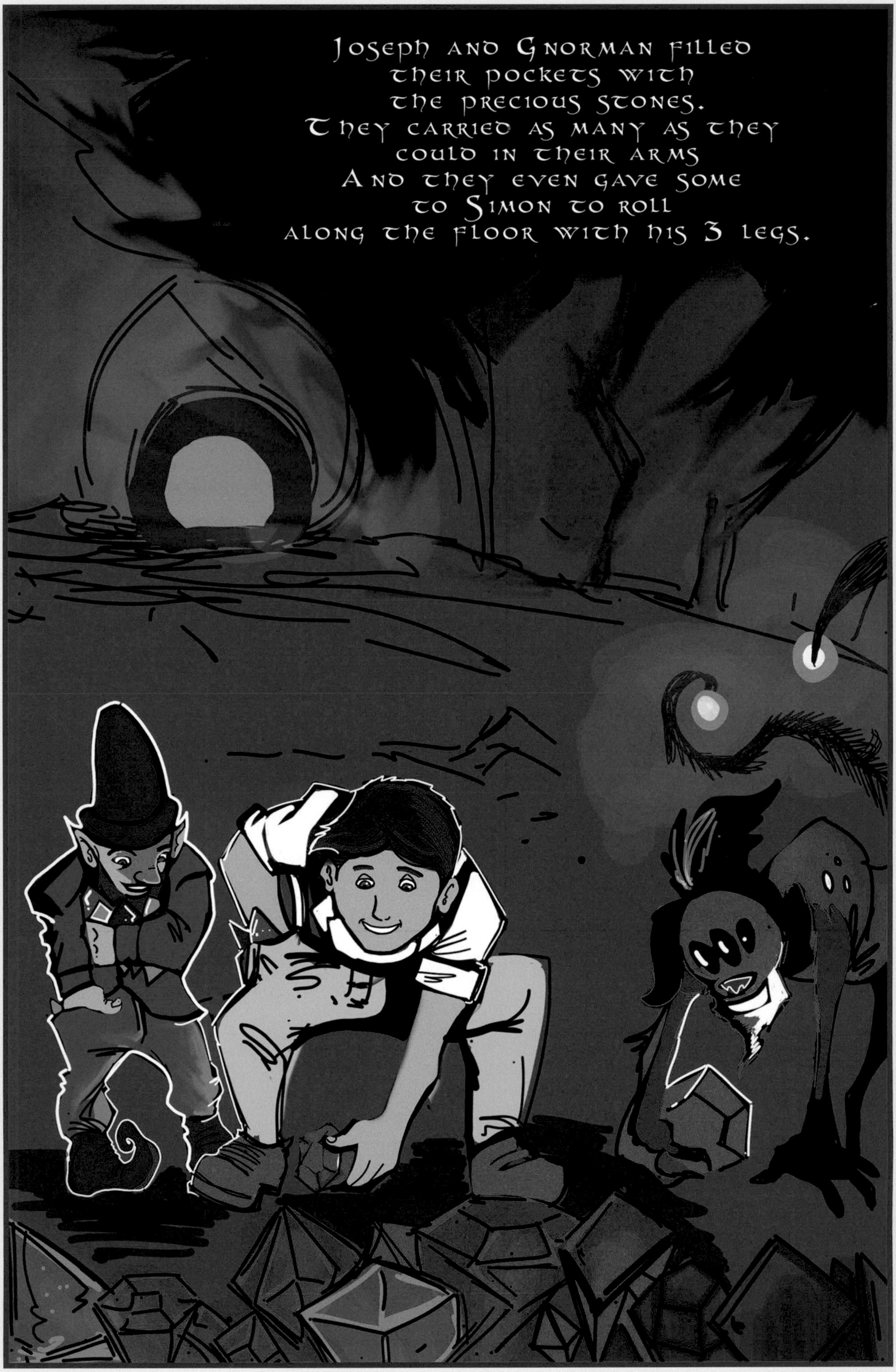
Joseph and Gnorman filled
their pockets with
the precious stones.
They carried as many as they
could in their arms
And they even gave some
to Simon to roll
along the floor with his 3 legs.

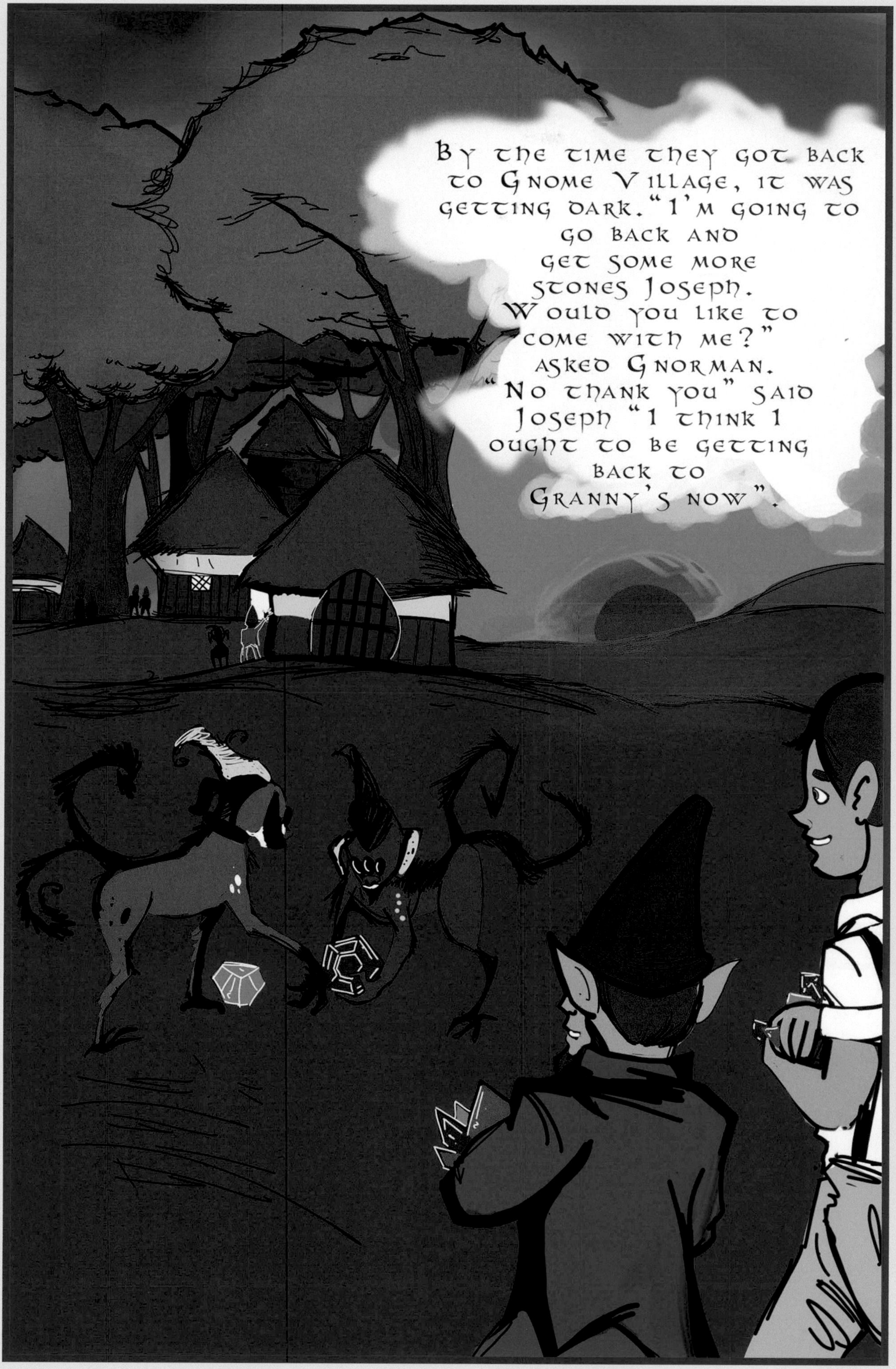
By the time they got back to Gnome Village, it was getting dark. "I'm going to go back and get some more stones Joseph. Would you like to come with me?" asked Gnorman. "No thank you" said Joseph "I think I ought to be getting back to Granny's now".

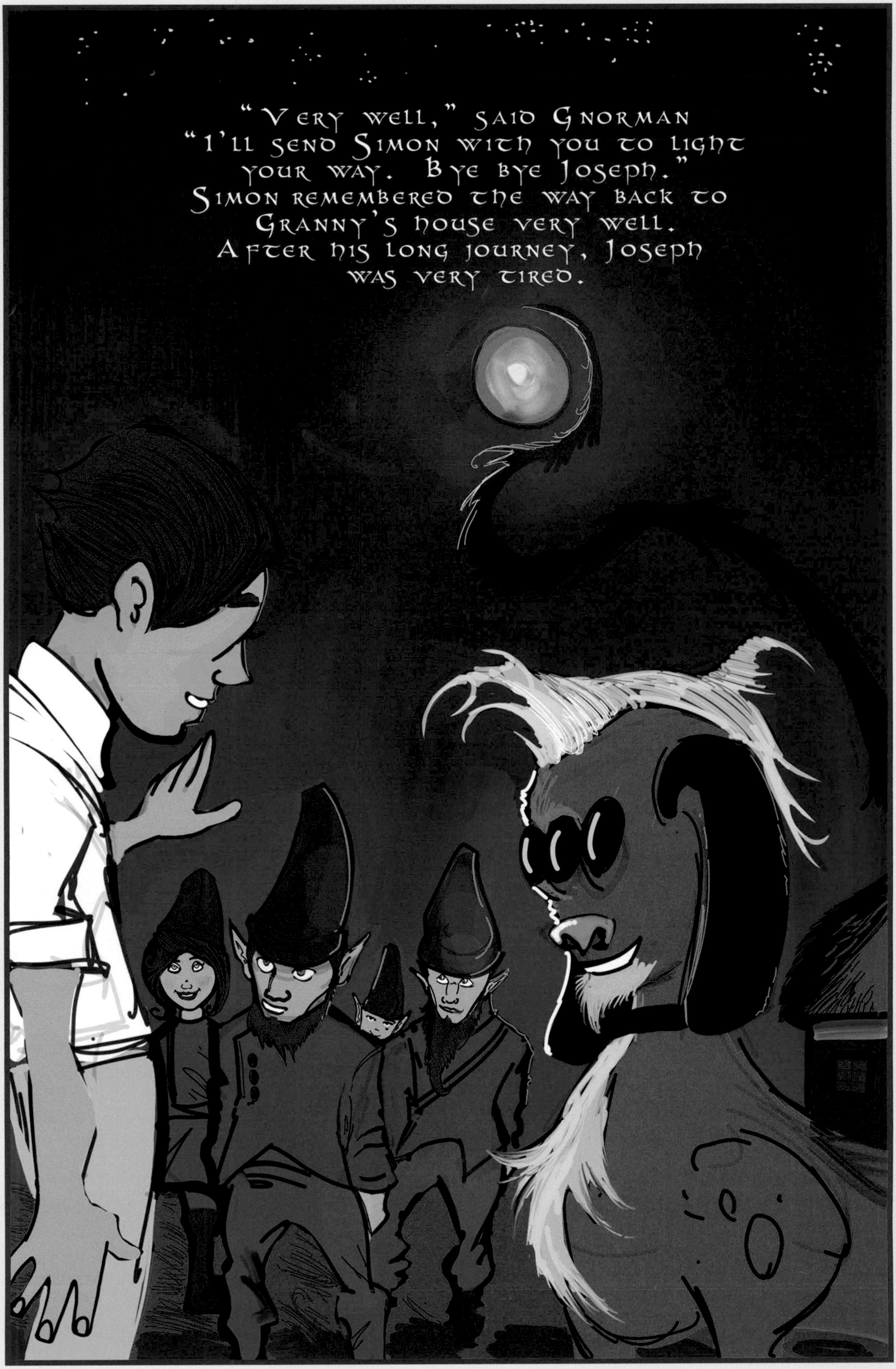
"Very well," said Gnorman
"I'll send Simon with you to light
your way. Bye bye Joseph."
Simon remembered the way back to
Granny's house very well.
After his long journey, Joseph
was very tired.

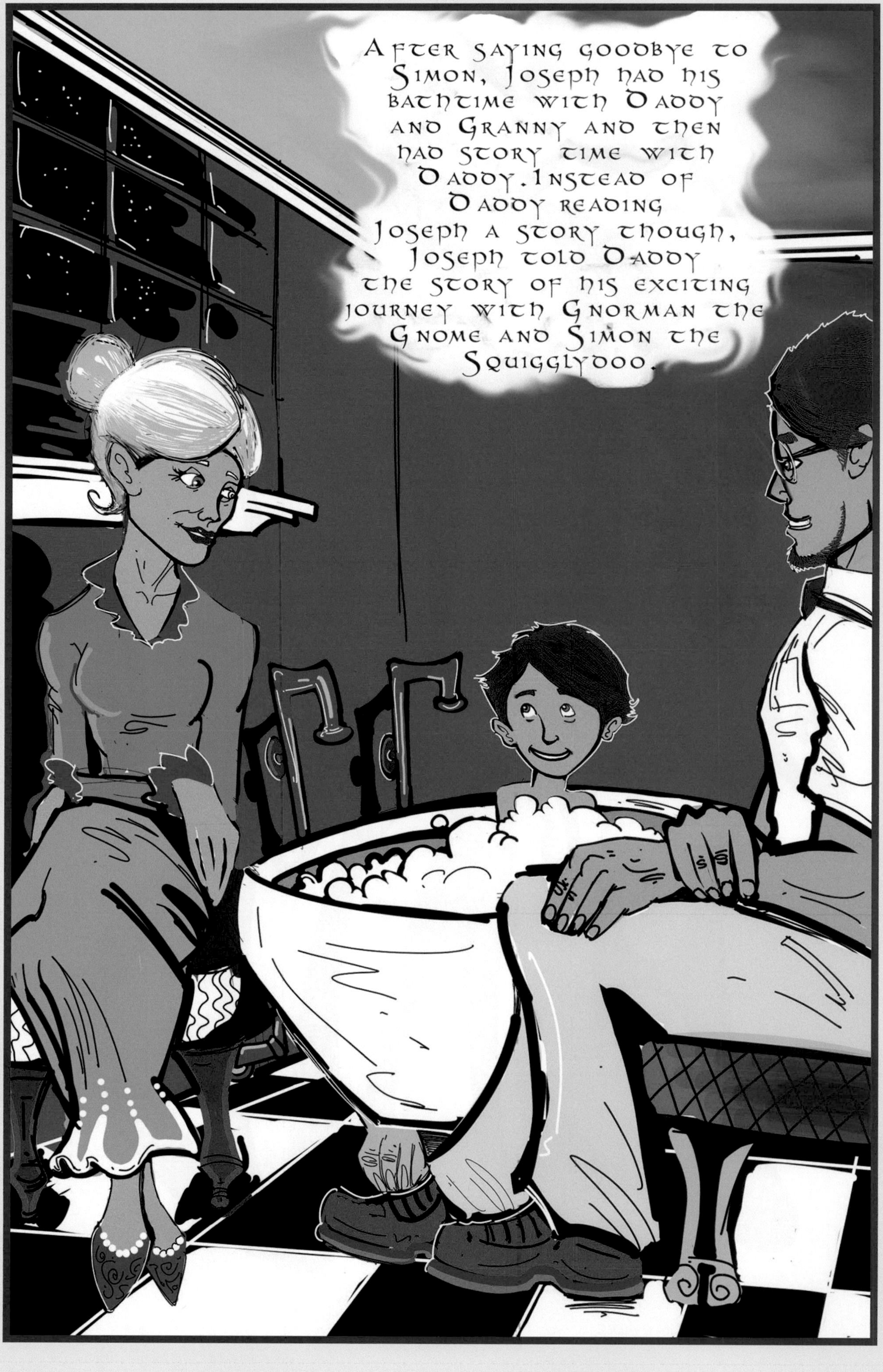
After saying goodbye to Simon, Joseph had his bathtime with Daddy and Granny and then had story time with Daddy. Instead of Daddy reading Joseph a story though, Joseph told Daddy the story of his exciting journey with Gnorman the Gnome and Simon the Squigglydooo.

THE END

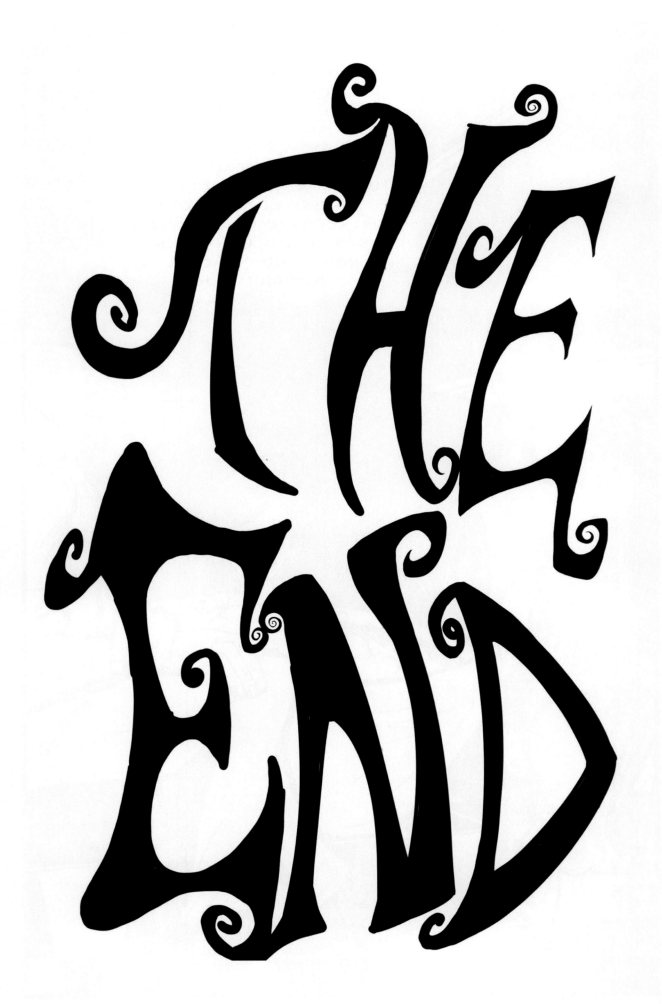

Printed in the United States
By Bookmasters